A Taste of Sanibel

Written by Karey Nicely
Photography by Laura Denick

the Peppertree Press
www.peppertreepublishing.com

For information regarding permission, call 941-922-2662
or contact us at our website: www.peppertreepublishing.com
or write to: The Peppertree Press, LLC., Attention: Publisher,
715 N. Washington Blvd., Suite B, Sarasota, Florida 34236

ISBN: 978-1-61493-976-4
Library of Congress:2024919546
Printed: September 2024

Manufactured in the United States of America

Dedication

I would like to dedicate my cookbook, A Taste of Sanibel,
to my husband, John. I love you to the moon and back.

Acknowledgment

I would like to thank my family for the wonderful memories I have cherished
and the recipes that inspired my cookbook. I would also like to thank Laura Denick
for bringing this book to life with her beautiful photographs and illustrations.

Table of Contents

Beach-Ready Belly-Filling Breakfasts

Appetizers and Tidbits

Fresh Salads and Sides

Fun-Filled Dinner Recipes

Cocktails and My Favorite Cupcake Recipe

Introduction

After living in the beautiful mountain town of Telluride, Colorado, I realized how much I missed the beach. It was time to choose between two very different lifestyles. Was I a ski bum at heart or a true beach bum? I knew deep within my heart that I belonged back at the beach. So my husband and I packed up our lives and moved to Sanibel Island in 2020. We immediately fell in love with the island.

My love for the water started as a very young child. I was lucky enough to grow up spending my summers at my grandparents' house on the Jersey shore. The memories I cherished most as a child revolved around the beach and family dinners in my grandmother's kitchen. I didn't know this at the time, but the memories ingrained in my heart and soul would be the inspiration to write this cookbook.

These recipes are a part of my past and my time spent living on Sanibel. I have had so much fun exploring and developing these recipes for you and your family. I hope when you and your family return home, you reach for A Taste of Sanibel. Whatever dish you decide to make, I hope it will bring you right back to this beautiful island that I am so lucky to call home. I thank my lucky stars every day.

Beach-Ready Belly-Filling Breakfasts

Beach House Eggs Benedict and Dreamy Creamy Hollandaise Sauce

What is the recipe for success? Just add Canadian bacon and my Dreamy Creamy Hollandaise Sauce. You can always buy the store packets of Hollandaise sauce, but I hope you venture out and try my easy blender Hollandaise sauce.

Ingredients *(Serves 2)*

4 English muffins, split
1 package Canadian bacon
4 eggs
Splash of white vinegar
Salt and pepper to taste
Fresh diced chives
My Easy Blender Hollandaise Sauce:
3 egg yolks
8 tbsp salted butter
1 tbsp lemon juice
1 tbsp hot water
Dash of cayenne pepper

Instructions

1. Cook bacon according to package directions. When bacon is cooked, cover with foil and set aside.
2. Set oven temperature to broil.
3. Place the muffins on a cookie sheet and set aside.
4. Melt the butter in the microwave.
5. Using the medium setting on your blender, add egg yolks and lemon juice. Blend for 30 seconds.
6. Slowly drizzle the hot butter into your egg and lemon juice mixture while the blender is still at a medium setting.
7. Slowly add the hot water to complete the sauce (don't forget the dash of cayenne pepper.)
8. Cover to keep warm, and set aside.
9. Bring a large pot of water and a splash of vinegar to a boil. Reduce heat to a medium simmer.
10. Crack one egg at a time into a bowl and then gently slip into the simmering water.
11. Allow each egg to simmer 3-5 minutes or until poached.
12. Using a slotted spoon, place each egg into a strainer.
13. Place English muffins in the oven. When the muffins start to brown, remove from oven.
14. Top each muffin with bacon, one egg, and Hollandaise sauce.
15. Add salt, pepper, and fresh chives. Enjoy!

Everything But the Kitchen Sink Frittata

Wondering what to do with all those leftovers? Make this delicious frittata.
I like to make my frittata in a cast iron pan. Using a cast iron pan adds such a
nice crust to the base of this dish, and the cast iron pan is completely oven safe.

Ingredients

(Serves 6)

10 eggs, beaten
1 lb cooked bacon, chopped
1 small head of broccoli, chopped
1 C onion, diced
1 bell pepper, diced
1 C cherry tomatoes, halved
1/4 C milk
1 C grated cheese
    (Monterey jack, gruyere, Swiss)
2 tbsp olive oil
2 tbsp butter
Salt and pepper to taste
Handful cilantro, chopped

Instructions

1. Preheat oven to 375 degrees.
2. In a large bowl, beat the eggs and whisk in the milk.
3. Stir in the grated cheese and set aside.
4. Cook bacon according to package directions. Once bacon is cool, roughly chop and set aside.
5. Place an oven-safe pan on medium-high heat and add the olive oil and butter.
6. Saute your veggies and season with salt and pepper.
7. Make sure your veggies are evenly distributed on the bottom of your pan.
8. Add the cooked chopped bacon to the veggie mix and then pour your egg/milk mixture on top.
9. Let rest on medium heat until your edges set.
10. Place your oven-proof pan into the oven and bake for 20 minutes or until cooked thoroughly.
11. Let your frittata rest for 5 minutes before slicing into pie-like slices.
12. Sprinkle with fresh cilantro and enjoy.

Lemony Eggs Benedict with Bacon on Avocado Sourdough Toast

Why do I have two different recipes dedicated to eggs benedict? Well, I am kind of obsessed with the dish. I just simply love the flavor combinations of the sourdough bread, the buttery consistency of the avocado, the sweet, smoky, salty flavor of bacon, and top it off with lemon and Hollandaise sauce. Well now, I'm in breakfast heaven.

Ingredients *(Serves 2)*

12 slices of cooked bacon
4 eggs
4 slices sourdough bread
1 avocado
1 lemon
1 tsp olive oil
Salt and pepper to taste

Ingredients for the Hollandaise Sauce

(See page 3 for my easy blender Hollandaise sauce)

Instructions

1. Cook the bacon according to package directions. Cover with foil and set aside.
2. Make the avocado spread by adding the meat of the ripe avocado into a bowl.
3. Add the lemon juice, olive oil, and salt and pepper. Mix this up to a chunky texture and set aside.
4. See page 3 to make the Easy Blender Hollandaise Sauce. Cover to keep warm and set aside.
5. Toast the sourdough.
6. Fry or poach the eggs.
7. Now it's time to assemble.
8. Spread the avocado spread on the toasted sourdough, layer a few bacon slices on top, add a poached of fried egg on top of the bacon, and add a generous amount of Hollandaise sauce to the top.
9. Top of your sandwich with a dash of salt and pepper and enjoy!

Overnight Muesli and Granola Treasure

I really enjoy the combination of granola and muesli, and muesli is packed with protein, so it will help keep your tummy feeling nice and full. You can add many different ingredients, so feel free to switch up your berries, nuts, and yogurt flavors. I like to make this the night before a fun-filled beach day.

Ingredients
(Serves 2)

1/2 C muesli
1/2 C granola
1 C Greek yogurt
1 1/2 tbsp chia seeds
1/4 C blueberries
1/4 C strawberries
1/4 C mixture of almonds, pecans, and pumpkin seeds
1 Florida orange, freshly squeezed
1 tbsp honey

Instructions

It's so easy! Add the granola, muesli, Greek yogurt, chia seeds, blueberries, strawberries, nut and seed mixture, fresh orange juice, and the honey to a jar with a lid and let sit overnight in the fridge. Stir together the next morning and enjoy!

Sand Dollar Buckwheat Pancakes Served with Sweet Lemon Sauce and Cracked Sea Salt

Buckwheat flour lends a lovely nutty flavor to these pancakes. Adding the delicate lemon sauce with the cracked sea salt is an easy way to bring something different and fun to the breakfast table. I like adding fresh seasonal berries if available.

Ingredients
(Serves 4)

Pancake Mix
1 C buckwheat flour
1 1/2 tsp sugar
1 tsp baking powder
1/4 tsp salt
1/4 tsp baking soda
1 1/4 C buttermilk
1 egg, beaten
1/4 tsp pure vanilla extract
1 tbsp unsalted butter

Lemon Sauce
3/4 C sugar
2 tbsp cornstarch
3 tbsp fresh lemon juice
2 egg yolks
3/4 C water
1 tsp lemon extract

Instructions for the Lemon Sauce

1. Combine the sugar and the cornstarch in a saucepan and whisk to combine.
2. Add the lemon juice, and stir.
3. Stir in the egg yolks, water, and lemon extract.
4. Continue cooking over medium heat until the mixture is thickened and smooth.
5. Keep warm and set aside until pancakes are done cooking.

Instructions for the Pancake Mix

1. In a large bowl, whisk the flour, sugar, baking powder, salt, and baking soda.
2. In a large bowl, using a mixer, beat the buttermilk, egg, and vanilla extract.
3. Pour the flour mixture into the buttermilk mixture; whisk until the batter is thick and smooth.
4. Let the batter rest for 5 minutes or until bubbles form.
5. Over medium heat, melt the butter on your griddle.
6. Drop the batter by large spoonfuls onto the griddle.
7. Cook 3-4 minutes per side.
8. Add the cracked sea salt after you drizzle the lemon sauce on your pancakes. Top with fresh seasonal berries if available.

Sandbar Streusel with Mixed Berry Coulis

What is coulis, you might be asking yourself? Well, it's just a fancy name for a delicious thin sauce made from pureed fruit. So dive right into this sandbar streusel and enjoy the flavor combinations that will please your entire family.

Ingredients for Cake

1 1/2 C flour
1 tsp baking powder
1/2 tsp baking soda
1/4 tsp salt
6 tbsp unsalted butter, softened
3/4 C sugar
1 egg and 1 egg yolk at room temperature
1 1/2 tsp pure vanilla extract
2/3 C plain Greek yogurt at room temperature
1/3 C buttermilk at room temperature
1 1/2 C mixed berries
1/4 C berry preserves (blueberry or blackberry)

Ingredients for Streusel Topping

3/4 C flour
1/2 C sugar
1/2 C brown sugar
1 tbsp cinnamon
1/4 tsp salt
6 tbsp unsalted butter, cold, cut into 1/4 inch pieces

Ingredients for Mixed Berry Coulis

1 C mixed berries, blueberries, raspberries, and blackberries
1/4 tsp orange zest
1/2 C sugar
1/4 C lemon juice
1/4 C water

Instructions for Preparing Cake Batter

1. In a medium bowl, whisk together the flour, baking powder, baking soda, and salt.
2. In a large bowl, using a mixer on medium speed, beat together until fluffy, the butter, sugar, egg (add the egg and egg yolk one at a time), and vanilla.
3. Slowly add the yogurt and buttermilk.
4. Reduce the blender speed to low and slowly add the flour mixture.
5. Stir in the berry mixture and the berry preserve.
6. Set aside.

Instructions for Preparing Streusel Topping

1. In a medium bowl, whisk together the flour, sugar, brown sugar, cinnamon, and salt.
2. Using your hands, press the butter into the mixture. The idea here is to form the crumble.

Preparing Mixed Berry Coulis

1. In a medium sized sauce pot over medium heat, combine the berries, orange zest, sugar, water, and lemon juice.
2. Bring to a boil and simmer for 8-10 minutes, stirring frequently. This can burn easily, so watch and stir often.
3. Remove from heat, cool, and purée with a blender.

Instructions

1. Preheat oven to 350 degrees.
2. Coat an 8-inch square baking dish with nonstick spray and dust lightly with flour.
3. Pour the cake batter into the pan. Top with the mixed berry coulis.
4. Sprinkle the streusel mix over the top. Bake the mixed berry coulis for 40 minutes or until a knife inserted comes out crumb-free.
5. Let stand for 10 minutes and enjoy.

The Original Uncle Hank

The first time I had the "Uncle Hank," I was in a small diner with some friends, and I was hooked. To be completely honest, I have no idea who Uncle Hank is or was (LOL), but the flavor combinations are delicious. My husband and I like to make these on Sunday mornings. Sometimes we switch up the cream cheese and use veggie cream cheese or chive cream cheese.

Ingredients

(Serves 2)

12 slices of bacon
8 oz whipped cream cheese
2 Everything bagels, sliced in half and toasted
2 large tomatoes, thinly sliced
Handful of fresh basil, roughly chopped
Salt and pepper to taste

Instructions

1. Preheat oven to 400 degrees.
2. Cook bacon according to package directions.
3. Thinly slice tomatoes and season with salt and pepper.
4. After the bacon is cooked, place the bacon on a paper towel to absorb the grease.
5. Toast the bagels.
6. After the bagels are toasted, spread the cream cheese, stack on the bacon slices, add the sliced tomatoes, and the chopped basil.
7. Season with more salt and pepper and enjoy!

Appetizers and Tidbits

1884 Lighthouse Tzatziki

Since I love snacking—I always have tzatziki in my fridge.
It is so refreshing to snack on after a day spent at the beach. I serve this
with fresh cut veggies, but it is such a treat to enjoy this dip with my
homemade salt and vinegar potato chips (see recipe on page 14).

Ingredients
(Serves 4)

1 cucumber, peeled and chopped
1 tbsp olive oil
2 tsp salt
1 tsp pepper
2 cloves minced garlic
1 ½ C full fat Greek yogurt
Juice of a lemon
Drizzle of olive oil

Instructions

1. In a large bowl, combine the yogurt, olive oil, salt, pepper, garlic, and lemon juice.

2. Add the chopped cucumbers, and stir until combined.

3. Set in refrigerator for an hour.

4. Drizzle olive oil and stir into the tzatziki until combined.

5. Serve with veggies or salt and vinegar chips.

FUN FACTS

The Sanibel lighthouse was built in 1884, and it was one of the first lighthouses built on the Gulf Coast.

The Captain's Salt and Vinegar Potato Chips

These tangy homemade chips are delicious with tzatziki dip, onion dip, or any kind of dip you like! I promise after making these chips, store bought chips will be history. They are so simple to make with only six ingredients (that you can pronounce). Store bought chips are loaded with sodium and certain ingredients that I have never heard of. But beware, these homemade chips are super addicting.

Ingredients

1 large russet potato
3/4 C white distilled vinegar
1 tbsp vinegar powder
2 tsp salt
2 tsp pepper
1 tbsp garlic powder

Instructions

1. Slice the potatoes thinly, about 1/10 inch thick.
2. Put the potato slices in a large bowl, and pour in the vinegar.
3. Soak for 45 minutes.
4. In a separate bowl, combine the salt, pepper, and vinegar powder.
5. Preheat oven to 400 degrees.
6. Line a cookie sheet with non-stick foil and lightly spray with cooking spray.
7. Remove potato slices from the bowl of vinegar and pat dry with a paper towel.
8. Bake the potato chips for 15 minutes per side, keeping an eye on your chips so they don't burn.
9. Once the chips are cooked and crispy, remove from the oven and let cool.
10. Toss your chips with the vinegar powder, salt, pepper and garlic powder.
11. Serve with your favorite dip and enjoy.

Gulf Shrimp Cocktail with Homemade Spicy Cocktail Sauce

In my family, we call shrimp the fruit of the sea. This is so refreshing after a day of fun and sun. For a little twist, I like to add a tiny splash of tequila to the spicy cocktail sauce.

Ingredients

1 lb medium gulf shrimp (deveined and peeled)
1 lemon
1 can of light beer

For the cocktail sauce:

1 C ketchup
2 tbsp fresh horseradish
1 tsp pepper
1 lemon juiced
1 tsp Worcestershire sauce
Dash olive oil
Dash of tequila (optional)

Directions for Cocktail Sauce

1. In a bowl, mix the ketchup, horseradish, pepper, lemon, Worcester sauce, olive oil, and a splash of tequila.
2. Chill in the fridge for one hour.

Instructions

1. Bring a can of beer to a full boil.
2. Add the shrimp, stirring often. Cook shrimp for 3 minutes.
3. Drain the shrimp in a colander, squeeze fresh lemon on top of shrimp, and chill for one hour.
4. Serve shrimp with cocktail sauce and enjoy.

Happy as a Clam Steamers

I hope you enjoy this dish as much as my family does. And don't forget
a fresh baguette for dipping. You will want to mop up every drop
of this velvety, garlicky white wine sauce.

Quick Tips for Cleaning and Storing

To remove the sand from the clams before cooking, cover the clams with cold water and a large dash of salt. Let the clams sit in the salty water for several hours. The combination of the salt and cold water will help the clam spit out the sand. Transfer clams to a clean surface and scrub with a brush and rinse again with cold water. Now, let's get cooking.

Ingredients

(Serves 4)

2 dozen Little Neck clams, rinsed and
  scrubbed
6 tbsp salted butter
2 tbsp fresh minced garlic
1 C white wine
2 tbsp fresh lemon juice
1 C chicken broth
1 tbsp red hot pepper flakes
2 tbsp chopped fresh flat parsley

Instructions

1. In a large skillet with a tight fitting lid, melt the butter over medium heat. Add the minced garlic and pepper flakes, stirring until fragrant (about 30 seconds).
2. Add the white wine, lemon juice, and chicken broth.
3. Bring to a boil.
4. Add the clams. Cover and steam until all the clams have opened (about 8 minutes).
5. Shake the pan occasionally during this part of the cooking process.
6. Discard any unopened clams.
7. Sprinkle fresh parsley and extra lemon if desired. Don't forget the baguettes.

Enjoy!

Oysters Rockefeller

When we first moved to Sanibel from Colorado, I was determined to learn how to make this classic dish. It took me a few tries to come up with this recipe, but I finally did it. I was so excited to share this recipe with my family, and they loved it, too. Everyone was shocked that you could make restaurant-quality Oysters Rockefeller right at home. This means you can, too!

Ingredients

(Serves 4)

12 shucked oysters
4 tbsp butter
2 shallots, minced
12 ounces fresh spinach
1/2 C white wine
1 lemon, juiced
1/2 C heavy whipping cream
3/4 C Romano cheese, grated
1/4 C Parmesan cheese, grated
1/4 C bread crumbs
Salt and pepper to tase
Flat-leaf parsley for garnish

Instructions

1. In a large pan, over medium heat, melt the butter and sauté the shallots for 3 minutes.
2. Add the fresh spinach and cook until wilted.
3. Add the wine, and stir occasionally.
4. After the wine has cooked off (about five minutes) add the lemon juice, heavy whipping cream, Romano cheese, Parmesan cheese, and the salt and pepper.
5. Bring to a boil and cook until the whipping cream has reduced by half.
6. Let the mixture cool and set in the refrigerator until mixture sets.
7. Preheat oven to 375 degrees.
8. Line a cookie sheet with foil and place one heaping tablespoon of the spinach mixture on top of each shucked oyster.
9. Sprinkle bread crumbs over oysters and bake for 15-20 minutes or until browned.
10. Serve with a squeeze of fresh lemon and a sprinkle of fresh flat-leaf parsley.

Mr. Salty's Grilled Pickles with a Sassy Dipping Sauce

What, grilled pickles? Absolutely! Serve these pickles alongside a sandwich, cheeseburger, or simply as a delicious snack.

Ingredients

1 jar of pickle spears
3-4 tbsp olive oil
1 C full fat plain Greek yogurt
1 tbsp fresh dill, minced
1 tbsp ground mustard powder
1 clove garlic, chopped
Splash of white vinegar
Pinch of celery salt
Salt and pepper
Dash of hot sauce

Instructions

1. In a medium size bowl, combine the yogurt, dill, mustard powder, garlic, white vinegar, celery salt, salt and pepper, and a dash of hot sauce.
2. Set in the refrigerator for an hour.
3. Preheat the grill to medium heat.
4. Pat pickles dry.
5. Brush the pickles with olive oil.
6. Place the pickles on the grill for 5-6 minutes per side or until grill marks appear.
7. Let the pickles cool and serve with the sassy sauce.

FUN FACTS

Sanibel Island has a 7,600 acre wildlife refuge named J.N. "Ding" Darling National Wildlife Refuge that you can drive, walk, or bike through.

Santiva's Beach Bread

My beach bread has a different spin on what you will find at the local restaurants here in SW Florida. Don't get me wrong, I love classic beach bread, which typically consists of lots of mozzarella cheese, bleu cheese, tomatoes, and garlic, but I add four different types of cheese in my beach bread that turned my version into a success! I hope you enjoy my spin on beach bread as much as I do!

Ingredients
(Serves 4)

One large loaf of Italian bread, preferably seeded
4 tbsp butter at room temperature
2 tbsp olive oil
2 tbsp mayonnaise
1 tbsp gorgonzola cheese
1/4 C grated parmesan cheese
1/4 C romano cheese
1/2 C grated fontina cheese
2 tbsp fresh chopped flat-leaf parsley
Salt and pepper to taste
Pinch of paprika
Pinch of red hot pepper flakes

Instructions

1. Set oven to broil.
2. Cut loaf of bread in half lengthwise.
3. Butter bread and drizzle olive oil over bread.
4. Broil in oven just until the edges are golden brown.
5. Remove from oven and set aside.
6. In a large bowl, mix together the mayonnaise, gorgonzola, parmesan, romano, and fontina cheese.
7. Add the paprika, red hot pepper flakes, and the salt and pepper.
8. Spread the mixture evenly on the bread. Watching closely, broil the beach bread. Make sure it does not burn.
9. When your beach bread is nice and crispy, top with flat leaf parsley and more paprika and enjoy!

Picnic Island Smoked Fish Dip

The best fish dip I ever had was in the Florida Keys. So when I tried
to make my own version, it was a little challenging, but I think
this is really quite tasty. This dip is perfect for a picnic,
a light snack, or even a cocktail party.

Ingredients
(Serves 2)

6 oz smoked salmon
3 tbsp mayonnaise
3 tbsp full fat Greek yogurt
1 tbsp vegetable cream cheese at
   room temperature
1 lemon, juiced
1 tbsp lemon zest
1 clove garlic, minced
1 tbsp cilantro, chopped
Dash of hot sauce
Dash of Worcestershire sauce
Salt and pepper to taste
Crackers for serving

Instructions

1. In a large bowl, combine the mayonnaise, yogurt, cream cheese, lemon, lemon zest, garlic, cilantro, hot sauce, Worcestershire sauce, and the salt and pepper to taste.

2. Flake the smoked salmon by hand and gently fold into your mixture. Refrigerate for an hour.

3. Serve with your favorite crackers.

Steamed Mussels in a Velvety Roasted Tomato Saffron Broth

Ingredients
(Serves 4)

1 – 28 oz can crushed tomatoes
3 cloves garlic, minced
4 tbsp olive oil
Salt and pepper to taste
1 onion, sliced thin
1 C dry white wine (Chardonnay works best)
1 C bottled clam juice
Pinch of saffron
3-4 pounds of mussels, scrubbed and debearded
1/4 C chopped flat-leaf parsley

Instructions

1. Preheat the oven to 350 degrees.
2. Toss the crushed tomatoes, salt and pepper, and garlic with 3 tbsp olive oil in an ovenproof roasting pan.
3. Roast the tomatoes for 30-40 minutes.
4. Transfer the roasted tomatoes and their juices to a food processor and purée until smooth.
5. Heat 1 tbsp olive oil in a large saucepan over medium heat.
6. Add the sliced onion, stirring often until opaque in color.
7. Add the wine until reduced by half.
8. Add the clam juice, saffron, and roasted tomato mixture, and bring to a boil.
9. Add the mussels and cover the pot with a lid.
10. Let the mussels cook for about 5-6 minutes.
11. Discard any mussels that don't open during cooking.
12. Stir in parsley and serve immediately.

Sun and Fun Charcuterie Board

When it comes to cheese making, summer is the season. Did you know that goats and sheep only produce milk in the spring and summer? The fresh grass helps give the cheese an even more delicious flavor. So make sure to add lots of goat and sheep cheese to your summer charcuterie board. The sky is the limit, so have fun when you are creating your sun and fun charcuterie board. You will be so impressed with how these warm weather cheeses can surely withstand the heat.

Ingredients

8 oz sheep's milk gouda
8 oz goat cheese
8 oz Camembert
8 oz bleu cheese
8 oz white cheddar cheese
2 packages of assorted crackers (I like fig and olive crisps)
16 oz variety of cured meats
8 oz large black olives
8 oz green olives
1 cup marinated artichokes
8 oz mini dill pickles
8 oz apricots
Fresh blueberries and raspberries for garnish

A Taste of the Tropics
Shrimp Ceviche Cocktail

This healthy, no-cook appetizer is packed with tons of fresh flavors and tastes so refreshing on a hot sunny day. I like to use Gulf shrimp when available.

Ingredients

1 lb Gulf Coast shrimp
3 large limes, juiced
1 C tomato, chopped
3/4 C cilantro, chopped
1/2 C fresh pineapple, chopped
1/2 C fresh mango, chopped
1 avocado, roughly chopped
1/4 C red onion, diced
1 jalapeno pepper, diced
1 tbsp garlic, minced
Salt and pepper to taste

Instructions

1. Bring a large pot of water to a boil.
2. Add the shrimp to the boiling water and cook just until pink, about 1 minute.
3. Drain the shrimp and let cool.
4. Once the shrimp are cool, chop into small pieces and set aside.
5. In another large bowl, combine the cooled shrimp, tomato, cilantro, pineapple, mango, avocado, onion, jalapeno, garlic, and salt and pepper.
6. Refrigerate for at least an hour and serve with tortilla chips.

Fresh Salads and Sides

Grandma Addie's Rib Doctor Baked Beans

This recipe is near and dear to my heart. It is also one of my favorites! My G-ma (her little nickname) would cook her rib doctor baked beans to celebrate the beginning of summer on Memorial Day the 4th of July, and of course on the bittersweet official closing of summer, Labor Day. For some reason, they tasted best to me on the 4th of July—I guess, because I knew we had almost two more months of summer fun on the Jersey shore. These baked beans are a real crowd pleaser, and they taste best with good old-fashioned hotdogs and hamburgers.

Ingredients

8 oz bacon, chopped
1 large red bell pepper, chopped
1 large green bell pepper, chopped
1 jalapeno, diced
2 tbsp olive oil
1 C dark brown sugar
1 C BBQ sauce (My G-ma liked to use hickory flavor)
1/3 C Maple syrup
28 oz pork and beans, drained
1 can of domestic beer

Instructions

1. Preheat grill to medium heat.
2. Cook bacon according to package directions. Drain on a paper towel and let cool.
3. Chop bacon.
4. In a large skillet, saute the onions, peppers, and jalapeno in olive oil until soft (about 3-5 minutes).
5. Lower heat to medium and stir in sugar, BBQ sauce, and the Maple syrup.
6. Bring mixture to a boil, stirring frequently. Once the mixture reaches a boiling point, stir and remove from heat.
7. Pour the pork and beans in a large reusable foil pan and add the mixture from Step 6. Add the bacon and pour a can of beer into the mixture and stir together.
8. Cover tightly with foil.
9. Cook on grill for 45 minutes, stirring three times.
10. Remove from grill and let cool for 15 minutes.
11. Remove foil and serve.

Grilled Iceberg Wedges with Tomato, Bacon, and Bleu Cheese

Have you ever tried grilling lettuce? Well, it is a must and to be put on your next to-do list. Don't get me wrong, I love a classic wedge salad, but the grill adds such a nice twist on an old classic dish.

Ingredients
(Serves 4)

8 oz. of bacon

4 oz. Roquefort bleu cheese

1/2 C buttermilk

3 tbsp sour cream

2 tbsp fresh lemon juice

Salt and pepper to taste

2 tbsp fresh diced chives

1 head iceberg lettuce trimmed. Discard outer leaves if necessary. Cut the lettuce into quarters

2 tbsp olive oil

Handful of cherry tomatoes

Instructions

1. Prepare grill for medium heat (350 degrees).
2. Cook bacon according to package directions. Set aside on a plate lined with paper towels.
3. Once the bacon has cooled, chop and set aside.
4. In a bowl, mash the bleu cheese with a fork. Add the buttermilk, sour cream, lemon juice salt, pepper, and stir in chives.
5. Drizzle olive oil on the lettuce wedges and season with salt. Place the wedges on the grill, cut side down, and grill for roughly 2 minutes. You'll want to see nice even grill marks. Turn and grill the other side, about 2 minutes more.
6. Transfer the grilled wedges to a platter and generously spoon the dressing on top.
7. Top with more bleu cheese, bacon, and cherry tomatoes over the wedge salad. Season with more salt and pepper if desired.

My Homemade Caesar Salad Dressing

When I was younger, I was a vegetarian for many years. I absolutely loved Caesar dressing. I thought to myself, *How could I possibly make this without Anchovies? Capers! Yes, capers.* They lend a similar saltiness that will compliment any Caesar dressing. My family was a little reluctant to try this "vegetarian friendly version," but I surely won them over. Try this with my mom's homemade croutons.

Ingredients

2 garlic cloves, chopped
2 tbsp capers, mashed
2 tbsp fresh lemon juice
1 tsp Dijon mustard
1 tsp Worcestershire sauce
1 C full fat plain Greek yogurt or regular mayonnaise
1/2 C fresh grated parmigiana
Salt and lots of pepper

Instructions

In a medium bowl, whisk together the garlic, capers, lemon juice, mustard, Worcestershire sauce, mayo or yogurt, parmigiana, and the salt and pepper. Taste and adjust to your liking. This can keep for up to 3 days in the fridge.

My Mom's Homemade Croutons

My mom used to make these when I was growing up. These cook up quickly, so keep an eye on them so they don't burn. Make sure you use a sturdy Italian bread—one day-old bread works best.

Ingredients

1 1/2 C stale Italian bread, cubed
1/4 C olive oil
3 cloves garlic, thinly sliced
2 tbsp Italian seasoning
Salt and pepper to taste
2 tbsp parmigiana

Instructions

1. Preheat oven to 375 degrees.
2. Place the cubed bread in a bowl.
3. Heat the olive oil and garlic in a pan until the garlic becomes fragrant, about 35 seconds.
4. Strain the garlic from the olive oil.
5. Drizzle the olive oil over the bread crumbs and toss with the Italian seasoning and salt and pepper.
6. Scatter on a baking sheet and bake for about 10 minutes.
7. When the croutons are golden brown, sprinkle with fresh parmigiana.

Nicely Done Brussel Sprouts

My original thoughts on brussel sprouts, to put it politely, no thank you. It wasn't until
I tried my husband's recipe that I changed my mind! So, nicely done John!
I hope this recipe converts you to a brussel sprout connoisseur.

Ingredients

1 lb fresh brussel sprouts
2 tbsp olive oil
2 tbsp garlic, chopped
Salt and pepper to taste
1 tbsp onion powder
1 tbsp red hot pepper flakes
1tbsp Italian seasoning
1 tsp lemon zest
2 tbsp parmigiana cheese

Instructions

1. Preheat oven to 425 degrees.

2. Line a rimmed cookie sheet with foil.

3. Prepare brussel sprouts by slicing off the nubby ends and remove any discolored or damaged leaves. Cut brussel sprouts in half from the flat base through the top.

4. In a large bowl, combine the brussel sprouts with the olive oil, garlic, salt and pepper, onion powder, pepper flakes, and Italian seasoning. Toss until the sprouts are lightly and evenly coated in the olive oil mixture.

5. Arrange the sprouts in an even layer with the flat side facing down.

6. Cook the sprouts until they are tender and golden brown on their edges (turning once) for about 30 minutes.

7. Remove the brussel sprouts and garnish with parmigiana cheese and fresh lemon zest.

Picnic Style Tortellini Salad

Don't skimp on the salt and pepper when making this crowd-pleasing salad.
Double the recipe if desired. Adding the fresh basil right before serving
adds a bright and pleasant flavor that won't disappoint.

Ingredients

1 lb small cheese tortellini
6 oz bag prosciutto
1/2 C small mozzarella balls
1 C bottled Italian dressing
1 tbsp Greek yogurt
1 C frozen peas
Splash of hot sauce
1 tbsp mustard
Pinch of red hot pepper flakes
Basil, a big handful, chopped
Salt and pepper to taste

Instructions

1. Cook tortellini according to package directions until done. Let cool and set aside.

2. Cook peas according to bag directions, drain, and set aside.

3. Whisk the Italian dressing, yogurt, hot sauce, mustard, pepper flakes, salt and pepper.

4. Add your cooked tortellini to the mixture and refrigerate for an hour.

5. In a small nonstick skillet, cook prosciutto over medium heat for 5-7 minutes or until crisp, stirring frequently.

6. Add mozzarella balls and crispy prosciutto to salad.

7. Add chopped fresh basil and serve.

Fun-Filled
Dinner Recipes

Whole Roasted Citrus Chicken with Onions, Potatoes, and Carrots

The first time I cooked this chicken dish, I completely surprised myself. The chicken turned out so moist and flavorful. The combination of the orange juice, key lime juice, and lemon juice adds such a bright and wonderful addition to this classic chicken dish. Enjoy!

Ingredients

(Serves 4-6)

1 whole chicken (3-4 pounds)

1/4 cup olive oil

2 tbsp lemon juice (save the rinds for stuffing the cavity)

2 tbsp lime juice (save the rinds for stuffing the cavity)

2 tbsp fresh Florida orange juice (Save the rinds for stuffing the cavity)

1 tsp paprika

1 tsp onion powder

1 tsp garlic powder

Salt and pepper to taste

1 tsp cumin

1 large onion, cut into thick slices

1 carrot, peeled and cut into chunks

4 garlic cloves, peeled and left whole

Instructions

1. Bring chicken to room temperature, about 30 minutes.

2. Preheat oven to 425 degrees.

3. Whisk in a bowl the olive oil, lemon juice, key lime juice, orange juice, paprika, onion powder, garlic powder, salt and pepper, and cumin.

4. In a large oven-safe dish, place the onions, carrots, and potatoes around the chicken.

5. Drizzle the marinade over the chicken, making sure to rub it around the to coat the skin.

6. Stuff the chicken cavity with the garlic cloves and leftover rinds from the oranges, lemons, and limes.

7. Place chicken in oven uncovered for 10-15 minutes or until it has a nice brown crisp on top. Keep an eye on this part as you don't want your chicken to burn.

8. After you are pleased with your nice brown crispy top, cover with non-stick aluminum foil. Cook chicken for 1 hour and 15 minutes. Insert a meat thermometer to check for an internal temperature of 165 degrees. Let chicken rest for 10 minutes before serving.

The Juan Ponce de León Cuban-Style Sandwich

With a little bit of planning, these sandwiches will surely please your family after a fun-filled beach day. Cuban bread can be difficult to find, so you can substitute with long soft French bread or Italian bread. Hawaiian dinner rolls are a great substitute, too.

Ingredients
(Serves 4)

1 loaf of French or Italian bread
2 tbsp Dijon mustard
2 tbsp butter
1 package Swiss cheese
1 package sweet deli ham
1 jar Giardiniera
1 small jar relish
1 lb boneless pork tenderloin
3 tbsp olive oil
1 tbsp garlic powder
1 tbsp lime juice
Salt and pepper to taste
One domestic beer
1/2 C chicken broth

Instructions

1. In a medium bowl, mix the olive oil, garlic powder, lime juice, and salt and pepper. Brush the mixture all over the pork.
2. Using a pot that will accommodate the roast, drizzle the olive oil in the pan over medium- high heat. Sear the pork for 3-4 minutes on each side, or until browned.
3. Add the beer and the chicken broth. Bring to a boil.
4. Decrease the heat to low and cook for 1 hour or until the pork shreds easily.
5. Now it's time to assemble the sandwiches.
6. Preheat the oven to 400 degrees.
7. Lightly toast the bread.
8. Once the bread is lightly toasted, spread a tablespoon of butter over the top and bottom of the bread.
9. Spread the mustard on the bread.
10. On the bottom piece of the bread, layer the cheese, Giardiniera, relish, ham, and shredded pork.
11. Now cover with foil and bake for 15-20 minutes. Serve hot.

FUN FACTS

Who is Juan Ponce de Leon? He is believed to have discovered Sanibel Island back in 1513!

Sunset Sizzlin' BBQ Pork Ribs

These ribs are sweet, tangy, and delicious. The best part is that the marinade is super easy to make. For the best flavor, marinade these ribs overnight.

Ingredients

(Serves 4)

2 lb pork short ribs
3 cloves garlic, minced
1/2 C soy sauce
1/2 C beer
1/4 C orange blossom honey
1 tbsp sesame oil
2 tbsp sesame seeds
1 tbsp Chinese chili paste
1 tbsp Sriracha
1 lime, squeezed
1/4 C mango juice or pineapple juice
Bunch of green onions, chopped
Salt and pepper to taste

Instructions

1. In a large bowl, whisk together the soy sauce, beer, honey, sesame oil, sesame seeds, chili paste, sriracha, lime juice, mango or pineapple juice, and salt and pepper.

2. Marinade the ribs overnight for best flavor.

3. Preheat oven to 275 degrees.

4. Wrap the ribs tightly in foil and place onto a cookie sheet. Bake for 1 hour.

5. Turn oven to 300 degrees, flip ribs, and cook for another hour.

6. Let the ribs cool to room temperature.

7. Heat grill to medium-high heat.

8. Keeping the foil on, place the ribs on the grill and BBQ for 8-10 minutes with the lid closed, checking every few minutes.

9. Flip ribs. Grill for another 6-7 minutes.

10. Baste with reserved marinade for optimal flavor and crispness.

11. Transfer the ribs to a cutting board. Cut into pieces and serve.

Spicy Fennel Meatballs with Homemade Spaghetti Sauce

Fennel is the star in this classic spaghetti and meatball recipe. The parmesan cheese rind is the runner-up in this dish. By adding the rind, you will add richness and depth to this classic dish. I like to give the meatballs a quick broil on both sides to give the outside a light golden-brown crust. To me, this is the ultimate comfort food, and don't forget to serve with a warm baguette.

Ingredients

(Serves 4)

1 lb ground chuck roast
1 clove garlic, minced
1/4 C onion, chopped
1 C Italian bread crumbs
1 egg, beaten
2 tbsp whole milk
Handful of fresh parsley, chopped
Handful of fresh basil, chopped
1/4 C grated parmigiana cheese
1 tbsp red hot pepper flakes
1 tbsp fennel seeds
Salt and pepper to taste

Sauce

1 – 28 oz can whole peeled tomatoes
1 – 28 oz can crushed tomatoes
1 – 6 oz tomato paste
3/4 C onion, chopped
1 tbsp garlic, minced
2 tbsp olive oil
1 tbsp Italian seasoning
1 bay leaf
1 tbsp red hot pepper flakes
Rind of parmigiana cheese block (optional)
Salt and pepper to taste
1/2 C red wine
Fresh basil, for serving
Fresh grated parmigiana, for serving
1 package of spaghetti noodles, cooked according to package directions

Instructions

1. Position oven rack in the middle of your oven, and preheat oven to broil.

2. In a large bowl, combine the ground chuck, garlic, onion, breadcrumbs, parsley, basil, parmigiana, fennel seeds, red pepper flakes, salt and pepper, milk, and egg.

3. Mix with your hands and form the meatballs, 1 1/2 inch in diameter. Place them on a cookie sheet lined with foil, 1/2 inch apart.

4. Once oven reaches a broil, place the meatballs on the middle rack until they are golden brown in color. Watch very closely so they don't burn.

5. Once the meatballs are golden brown, remove from oven and set aside on a plate lined with paper towels (you will want to absorb some of the grease.)

6. In a large saucepot over medium heat, sauté the garlic in the olive oil for 40 seconds. Make sure you don't burn the garlic.

7. Add onions and sauté until the onion is translucent.

8. Stir in both 28 oz cans of tomatoes, tomato paste, Italian seasoning, salt and pepper, bay leaf, pepper flakes, and red wine.

9. Add the meatballs to the sauce.

10. Cover the sauce with the lid, but slightly cracked.

11. Reduce heat to low and simmer for 90 minutes. Stir every 15-20 minutes.

12. Add the parmigiana rind during the last 30 minutes of cooking and adjust seasoning as needed.

13. Discard rind once you are ready to serve.

14. Cook spaghetti according to package directions.

15. Strain and serve hot.

16. Add desired amount of sauce and meatballs to each bowl.

17. Garnish with fresh basil and extra parmigiana. Serve with a fresh baguette.

Southwest Citrus Orange Chicken

This dish will give takeout food a run for its money. This dish is sweet, tangy, and has all of the savory flavors I love. Fresh oranges are the key to making this delicious marinade. I like to serve this over a bed of jasmine rice.

Ingredients for the Sauce

1 1/2 C water
2 tbsp fresh orange juice
1 tbsp orange zest
1/4 C fresh lemon juice
1/3 C rice vinegar
1/2 tbsp soy sauce
1 tbsp honey
1/2 tsp fresh ginger root, grated
1/2 tsp minced garlic
1 tbsp red pepper flakes
Sesame seeds for garnish

Ingredients for the Chicken

2 boneless, skinless, chicken breasts, cut up into 1/2 inch pieces
1 C flour
1/4 tsp salt
1/4 tsp pepper

Instructions

1. Combine the water, orange juice, lemon juice, rice vinegar, and soy sauce in a saucepan over medium low heat.
2. Stir in the orange zest, honey, ginger, garlic, red pepper flakes, and bring to a boil.
3. Remove from the heat and let cool for 20 minutes.
4. Place the chicken pieces into a plastic baggie, and when the marinade has cooled, pour 1 cup of the marinade into the bag. Save the remaining sauce and set aside.
5. Marinade the chicken in the fridge for at least 3 hours or overnight.
6. In a large bowl, add the flour, salt, and pepper.
7. Add the marinated chicken pieces and coat lightly, shaking off any excess flour.
8. Heat olive oil in a large skillet over medium heat. Place the chicken in the skillet and brown on both sides.
9. Drain the chicken on a plate lined with paper towels and cover with foil to keep warm.
10. In a clean skillet, add the sauce and bring to a boil.
11. Using a whisk, whisk 2 tbsp water and cornstarch until combined and thickened.
13. Reduce the sauce to a medium heat and add the chicken pieces.
14. Simmer on low heat for 10-15 minutes.
15. Serve over a bed of jasmine rice and garnish with sesame seeds.

San Cap's Tropical Mango Chicken

This chicken dish has the perfect balance of sweet and spicy. The mango lime marinade will caramelize the chicken perfectly, and the spice combination is just right. So when you are feeling like a tropical BBQ experience, this dish will be your new go-to.
I like to serve this dish alongside rice and fresh steamed broccoli.

Ingredients
(Serves 4)

1 1/2 pound chicken thighs (I like to use bone in and skin on)
1 Cup mango puree
3 tbsp key lime juice
2 tbsp olive oil
1 tbsp fish sauce
1 tbsp honey
1 tbsp hot chili sauce
1 clove garlic, minced
1 tbsp soy sauce
2 tbsp chopped cilantro
1 tsp red pepper flakes
1/2 tsp salt
1/2 tsp pepper

Instructions

1. Combine the mango puree, key lime juice, fish sauce, olive oil, honey, hot chili sauce, garlic, shallot, salt, pepper, and red pepper flakes in a large plastic resealable baggie. Add chicken and marinate at least 3 hours, or overnight if possible.

2. Preheat your grill to medium heat.

3. Once the grill is ready, remove the chicken from the marinade and place on the grill.

4. Grill chicken for 10 minutes per side or until done. Baste the chicken with the leftover marinade. Grill chicken until it has reached an internal temperature of 165 degrees. Tent the chicken with foil and let cool for 5 minutes.

5. While chicken is cooling, bring the remaining marinade to a boil in a small saucepan. Rapidly boil the marinade for at least 5 minutes.

6. Serve chicken with the mango sauce and chopped cilantro.

FUN FACTS

The Bailey Matthews Shell Museum is the only shell museum in the entire country!

Rose's Rigatoni alla Vodka Sauce

Many years ago, I went to a neighbor's house for dinner and tried vodka sauce for the first time—it was delicious. I asked Rose to write down the recipe, and I have savored her recipe for all these years. I lost touch with Rose, so I hope she is healthy, happy and still cooking her sauce! This dish is perfect for pasta night with family or friends.

Ingredients

(Serves 4)

1 box Rigatoni
2 tbsp olive oil
2 tbsp butter
1/3 C onion, diced
2 cloves garlic, diced
1/2 C vodka
1 – 28 oz can of diced tomatoes
1 – 8 oz can of tomato sauce
1 C heavy cream
1 tsp salt
1 tbsp red hot pepper flakes
Fresh grated parmigiana cheese for serving
Fresh parsley and basil, roughly chopped

Instructions

1. Slowly bring a large pot of salted water to a boil.
2. Heat a large pan over medium heat. Add olive oil and butter.
3. Once the butter has melted, sauté the onion until very soft, about 10 minutes.
4. Add garlic and cook for 2 minutes.
5. Pour in the vodka and cook for 2-3 minutes, stirring frequently.
6. Add tomato sauce, diced tomatoes, heavy cream, salt, and red hot pepper flakes.
7. Simmer for 15 minutes or until sauce has slightly thickened, stirring occasionally.
8. This is a good time to add your pasta to the boiling water and cook according to package directions.
9. While pasta is cooking, keep the sauce on low and stir frequently.
10. Drain pasta in a colander.
11. Divide pasta into bowls and add the vodka sauce.
12. Add parmigiana cheese and the fresh herbs.

Pierside Seafood Lasagna

This delicious dish is loaded with shrimp, bay scallops, and crabmeat. This lasagna is so rich and satisfying. It's a must-make dinner for any seafood lover.

Ingredients

1 white onion, diced
2 tbsp olive oil
2 tbsp butter
1/2 C butter, brought to room temperature
1/2 C chicken broth
8 oz clam juice
1 lb bay scallops
1 pound shrimp, peeled and deveined
8 oz crabmeat
1 C all-purpose flour
1 1/2 C whole milk
Salt and pepper to taste
1 C heavy whipping cream
1/2 C shredded parmigiana
1 C mozzarella
1 package uncooked lasagna noodles
Fresh basil for garnish
Fresh flat-leaf parsley for garnish

Instructions

1. Preheat oven to 350 degrees
2. In a large pan, sauté the onion in the butter until translucent.
3. Stir in chicken broth and clam juice, bringing to a boil.
4. Add scallops, shrimp, and crabmeat. Cook for 4-5 minutes, stirring frequently.
5. Using a slotted spoon, scoop seafood into a bowl and cover with foil and set aside.
6. In another large pan, melt the remaining butter, add milk, and whisk in flour until smooth.
7. Whisk in remaining liquid from the seafood.
8. Add salt and pepper.
9. Whisk for 2 minutes or until thickened.
10. Remove from heat. Stir in heavy cream and 1/4 of the parmigiana
11. Stir 3/4 C of the white sauce into seafood mixture.
12. Spread 1/2 C white sauce into a greased 13x9 baking dish.
13. Top with lasagna noodles.
14. Spread half the seafood mixture and 1-1/4 C sauce.
15. Repeat layers, ending with noodles on top.
16. Top with remaining sauce and mozzarella cheese.
17. Bake covered in foil for 30 minutes or until bubbly.
18. Remove foil and bake until golden brown, usually another 15 minutes.
19. Let stand for 20 minutes before serving.
20. Garnish with fresh herbs.

"On Island" Limoncello Shrimp

In my experience, limoncello is always served as an after-dinner drink.
Who knew you could cook with it! The flavor combinations of the limoncello,
cream, and butter are pleasantly sweet. I like to spice this dish up by adding red
hot pepper flakes. Try this served with a warm crusty baguette.

Ingredients

1 pound gulf shrimp, peeled and cleaned
2 cloves garlic, minced
1 lemon, zested
1 tbsp herbs de Provence
3/4 C limoncello
3 tbsp butter
1/2 C heavy cream
1 tbsp red hot pepper flakes
1 tbsp chopped flat-leaf parsley
1 tbsp fresh basil
Salt and pepper to taste
One warm crusty baguette

Instructions

1. In a large sauté pan, mix the olive oil, garlic, lemon zest, red hot pepper flakes, salt and pepper, and herbs de Provence. Sauté for one minute.

2. Add the shrimp and cook 3-4 minutes, stirring until cooked through.

3. Remove the shrimp and set aside. Cover with foil to keep warm.

4. In another saucepan, cook limoncello on high heat until reduced to 1/4 cup.

5. Remove from heat and whisk in butter and cream.

6. Pour this over the shrimp and add flat-leaf parsley and fresh basil.

7. Adjust seasoning, if desired, and serve with a warm crusty baguette.

No-Fail Island-Style Oven-Baked Pork Tenderloin

You'll be hanging loose with my no-fail grilled pork tenderloin dish.
This dish can surely take the heat! If time permits, I
marinate this pork dish overnight for best flavor.

Ingredients
(Serves 6)

2 lb pork tenderloin
1/2 C soy sauce
1/4 C fresh Florida orange juice
1/4 C pineapple juice
2 tbsp key lime juice
2 tbsp honey
1 tbsp hot chili sauce
1 tbsp ketchup
1 tsp ground mustard powder
1 tbsp fresh grated ginger
2 cloves garlic, minced

Instructions

1. Combine in a large plastic resealable baggie the soy sauce, orange juice, pineapple juice, key lime juice, honey, hot chili sauce, ketchup, mustard powder, grated ginger, and minced garlic.

2. Add the pork tenderloin to the marinade and refrigerate overnight.

3. Preheat the grill to medium heat. Grill the tenderloin for about 8-10 minutes per side.

4. When the tenderloin is cooked, tent with foil and let rest for 10 minutes before cutting into it. Serve warm.

Mr. Crabby's Hotdog with Crabby Mac Salad

It's time to teach that old hotdog some new tricks. This is such a fun and easy dish to make. The crabby mac salad will take your hotdog to a whole new level of deliciousness.

Ingredients

(Serves 4)

Hot Dogs

4 hotdogs
4 pretzel buns
1 lemon
1 pinch Old Bay seasoning

Mr. Crabby's Mac Salad

1 cup elbow macaroni

3/4 C mayonnaise
8 oz can crabmeat, drained and flaked
1/3 C red bell pepper, chopped
2 stalks chopped celery
2 tbsp chili garlic sauce
2 tbsp lemon juice
1 tbsp fresh chopped dill
1 tbsp fresh chopped chives
1 tsp red hot pepper flakes
Salt and pepper and serve with a pickle

Instructions

Mr. Crabby's Mac Salad

1. Bring a large salted pot of water to a boil.
2. Cook the elbow macaroni in the boiling water according to package directions, stirring occasionally.
3. Drain and rinse macaroni and set aside.
4. In a large mixing bowl, add mayonnaise, crabmeat, celery, red bell pepper, chili garlic sauce, lemon juice, dill, chives, pepper flakes, salt and pepper.
5. Stir the elbow macaroni into the mixture.
6. Adjust seasoning if needed.
7. Chill for one hour.

Hotdogs

1. Grill hotdogs until golden brown.
2. Place hotdog on the pretzel bun, and squeeze fresh lemon and add a pinch of Old Bay seasoning.
3. Scoop 2 heaping tbsp of Mr. Crabby's Mac Salad on top of your hotdog. Serve with a crisp dill pickle.

Let the Sun Shine Lemon Zest Rigatoni

Making a roux sounds intimidating, but it's really just a fancy word to describe a mixture of equal parts of flour and butter cooked together. This roux adds a richness to the dish, and it will coat those tasty little tubes of pasta perfectly. I love how the lemon adds a bright and refreshing taste, too.

Ingredients

(Serves 4)

1 box rigatoni
2 tbsp butter
1/2 tbsp flour
1 clove garlic, minced
1/4 C white wine
2 tsp lemon juice
1 lemon, zested
1 C heavy cream
1/4 C parmigiana cheese
1/4 C Romano cheese
Salt and pepper to taste
Sprinkle of red hot pepper flakes
Fresh basil and extra cheese for garnish

Instructions

1. Bring a large pot of salted water to a boil, and cook pasta according to package directions.
2. Add the butter to a large saute pan and melt over medium heat.
3. Sprinkle the flour into the melted butter and whisk frequently for 1-2 minutes.
4. Add the garlic, wine, lemon juice, and lemon zest, and let simmer for 1 minute.
5. Whisk in the cream and cook until sauce has thickened, about 2-3 minutes.
6. Stir in the cheese and remove from the heat.
7. Season with salt and pepper, and sprinkle with pepper flakes.
8. Drain the pasta, add to the saute pan, and toss until coated well.
9. Garnish with extra cheese and fresh basil.

Darn Good Mahi Tacos with Spicy Mango Salsa

If you ask me, anytime is the time for tacos and savory salsa! The mango salsa combines heat and sweet for a mouth-watering taco experience.

Ingredients
(Serves 4)

Salsa

1 small red onion, diced
6 plum tomatoes, chopped
1 jalapeño peppers, diced
3 tbsp fresh minced cilantro
2 limes, juiced
1 tbsp of your favorite hot sauce
1 tbsp salt
2 tbsp orange blossom honey

Instructions

Combine the mango, red onion, plum tomatoes, jalapeños, cilantro, lime juice, hot sauce, salt, orange blossom honey, and gently stir. Adjust seasoning if desired. Set in fridge for 1 hour before serving.

Ingredients

Tacos

4 mahi filets skinless, 6 ounces each
1 tsp chili powder
1 tsp ground cumin
1 tsp paprika
1 tsp onion powder
1 tsp garlic powder
2 tbsp lime juice
2 tbsp pineapple juice
Dash of your favorite hot sauce
Salt and pepper to taste
3 tbsp olive oil

Instructions for assembling:

6 corn or flour tortillas

Mango salsa (see recipe above)

1 C chopped cabbage

1/2 cup fresh cilantro

1/2 cup thinly sliced radish

1 fresh jalapeno pepper, thinly sliced

Sour cream

Your favorite hot sauce

Lime wedges

Instructions

1. Make the marinade by mixing together in a medium bowl the chili powder, cumin, paprika, onion powder, garlic powder, lime juice, pineapple juice, hot sauce, salt and pepper, and olive oil.

2. Add the mahi to the marinade.

3. Let marinade for 1-3 hours.

4. Heat your grill to medium-high heat.

5. Grill the fish, carefully turning or until opaque and just cooked through, about 8 minutes total. Discard marinade.

6. Heat the tortillas directly on the grill.

7. Place the cooked fish in the warmed tortilla and top with mango salsa, cabbage, fresh cilantro, radishes, sliced jalapenos, and hot sauce.

8. Add a dollop of sour cream if desired, and garnish with fresh lime.

Chillin' and Grillin' Flat Iron Steak with Chimichurri Sauce

This recipe is a must during the summertime or anytime—really! Once you light the grill and the steak starts sizzling, your mouth will start watering for this dish. I just love the fresh herbs used in this marinade, too! Try to marinate overnight for best flavor.

Ingredients

(Serves 4)

1 1/2 lb flat iron steak
1/2 C olive oil
1/4 C red wine vinegar
1 C cilantro, chopped
1/4 C mint, chopped
1 C parsley, chopped
2 cloves garlic, minced
1 tsp cumin
1 tsp paprika
1 tbsp red hot pepper flakes
Juice of 1 lime
Salt and pepper
Splash of domestic beer

Instructions

1. In a large bowl, combine olive oil, vinegar, cilantro, mint, parsley, garlic, cumin, paprika, pepper flakes, lime, salt and pepper and splash of beer.

2. Add the meat to the marinade.

3. Marinade the meat in the fridge overnight.

4. Heat the grill to medium-high heat.

5. Once the grill is hot, add the meat and BBQ for 8-10 minutes with the lid open.

6. Flip meat and cook through, about another 8 minutes.

7. Meanwhile, in a medium sauce pot, bring the remaining marinade to a boil and let simmer on low for 15 minutes.

8. Once the meat is cooked to your liking, let it rest, covered for 10 minutes.

9. Thinly slice the steak across the grain, spoon the marinade over the meat, and serve.

Cocktails and My Favorite Cupcake Recipe

Boat Dock Punch

This punch may seem a bit intimidating to make, but it's very simple and delicious. Remember that muddling the lemon peels and the sugar together is the key to making this punch pop! Cheers!

Ingredients

750 ml rose sparkling wine
1/2 C vodka
4 lemon peels
1/2 C sugar
12 oz fresh grapefruit juice
12 oz fresh orange juice
2 oz grenadine
Orange slices for garnish

Instructions

1. In a bowl, muddle the lemon peels with the sugar.
2. Discard lemon peels from sugar.
3. In a large punch bowl filled with ice, add the vodka, grapefruit juice, orange juice, and grenadine.
4. Add the sugar to the punch bowl.
5. Add the sparkling rose to the punch bowl.
6. Stir well to combine.
7. Divide into glasses and garnish with orange slices.

Perfectly "Peared" Cocktail

This perfectly "peared" cocktail is one of my favorites.
So sit back, relax, and drink in good measure.

Ingredients

2 oz spiced rum
2 oz pear puree
1 tbsp simple syrup
1/2 lemon, juiced
1 ginger beer
Lime wedge for garnish

Instructions

1. In a cocktail shaker, combine the rum, pear puree, simple syrup, and lemon juice, and shake it up.
2. Pour over a glass full of ice and top off with the ginger beer.
3. Garnish with a lime.

A Very Luscious Slushy Cocktail

When the sky turns pink, it's time for a drink! This cocktail is so refreshing and easy to make. I like to serve this drink in a hurricane-style glass with a big chunk of pineapple.

Ingredients

(Serves 4)

5-6 C ice cubes
1/2 C white rum
2 1/2 C fresh pineapple juice
1/4 C grenadine
1/4 C shiraz
1/2 C fresh lemon juice
3 tbsp Aperol
Pineapple wedge for garnish

Instructions

In a blender, blend the ice, rum, pineapple juice, grenadine, shiraz, lemon juice, and Aperol. Blend until slushy. Serve in a glass with the pineapple wedge.

The Whitecap

Sanibel isn't exactly known for its cold winter nights, but every now and again we have some chilly nights, especially around the holidays. This cocktail is perfect for making everyone's spirits bright on those unusual chilly nights. You will want to top off this decadent, creamy and rich cocktail with whipped cream and a cherry.

Ingredients
(Serves 2)

2 oz coffee flavored liquor

3 oz vodka

2 oz salted caramel syrup

3 oz heavy whipped cream

Cherries for garnish

Instructions

1. Using a cocktail shaker, fill half way with ice and add the coffee liquor, vodka, caramel syrup, and heavy cream.

2. Shake to combine.

3. Pour into a glass and serve with whipped cream and a cherry on top.

The Tropical Rainstorm

Cherished summer nights on Sanibel call for a delicious hand-crafted cocktail.
This cocktail is a tribute to the beautiful island that I am so lucky to call home.

Ingredients

(Serves 4)

3 C fresh pineapple juice
3 C fresh orange juice
Splash of grenadine
1 tbsp fresh lime juice
1/2 C white rum
1/2 C dark rum
3 tbsp Campari
Orange wedges and maraschino
   cherries for garnish

Instructions

1. Mix pineapple juice, orange juice, lime juice, rum, dark rum, and Campari in a pitcher. Cover and chill for 3 hours.
2. Divide among ice-filled glasses.
3. Garnish with an orange wedge and maraschino cherries.

Zesty Guava Cream Cheese Cupcakes

My husband, John, told me about this cupcake recipe. Much to my surprise, he used to bake these long before we were married. Who knew that guava and cream cheese would be one of my new flavor combinations. These cupcakes will steal the show at your next party or special occasion.

Ingredients

(Serves 24)

1 box white cake mix
2 1/4 C guava nectar juice
3 eggs
1/4 C vegetable oil
1 tsp vanilla extract
1 tsp lime zest
1/4 C guava jelly
1/2 tsp red food coloring
1/2 tsp green food coloring
Store bought cream cheese frosting
Sprinkles for garnish

Instructions

1. Preheat oven to 350 degrees.
2. In a sauce pan, bring the guava nectar to a simmer until reduced by half.
3. Remove from heat and let cool.
4. In a large bowl, using an electric mixer, add the cake mix, cooled guava nectar, eggs, vegetable oil, vanilla extract, lime zest, and guava jelly.
5. Blend on medium speed until smooth.
6. Add the food coloring until desired color (should be slightly pink).
7. Divide mix into cupcake liners.
8. Bake for 20-25 minutes.
9. In a large bowl, mix the frosting with the green food coloring (should be a light greenish color).
10. Once cupcakes have cooled, spread frosting over the cupcakes and garnish with sprinkles.

Printed in the USA
CPSIA information can be obtained
at www.ICGtesting.com
JSHW041229071124
73041JS00005B/17